Quivering Steps
Harlie McCloud

Copyright © 2019 Harlie McCloud

All rights reserved. No part of this book may be reproduced or transmitted in any form or by any means, electronic or mechanical, including photocopying, recording or by any information storage and retrieval system, without permission in writing from the publisher.

Luna Tuna—Cleveland, OH
ISBN: 978-0-578-62292-7
Quivering Steps | Harlie McCloud
Available Formats: eBook | Paperback distribution

Dedication

For those who gave me the harsh hardships I had to conquer to learn discipline, strength, and respect for myself *thank you.*
For those who loved me when I wasn't lovable
I love you, thank you.
For those who appreciated the good in me
For those who stood by me because:
"If you can't handle someone at the worst points, no one deserves them at their best."
It took a long time to get here.
Last but not least for those who are reading this right now thank you for believing in me at my best.

Introduction

They say "You only live once..." False.
You live every day, you only die once.

The time I have spent in my life with denial has now become a settling solitude, knowing that I can bring my words to life. I have always written them in what others would call a terrifying silence, but a silence I was naturally comfortable with because in my head there was never a dull moment.

Circumstances of one's birth are sometimes irrelevant, it is what you do with the deceptions and gifts of life that determines who you are. There is a fine line between what you think you know, and what you will potentially learn with life experiences.

This in which we all do... Making unconscious decisions to later learn from the mistakes and life lessons. This helps us revoke ourselves in the next scenario, provoking ourselves into a conscious decision. Nobody should ever feel disrupted for making hard earned mistakes. It's only taking us closer to where we truly belong. As the quote goes "We live and we learn."

If there is one thing I can say I have learned out of all of my trials and lessons to be true in life, Is that there really are no accidents or mistakes.

Substantially every being, creature, or living thing, will inevitably lose something that is important to them, experiencing grief and loss in so many different ways whether we want to or not. The saying "Everything is just temporary." has made me think a lot. I have come to believe it's true because the pain won't last forever, and the struggles will fade. If you live life on the thought that you will lose something, or everything, then you already have nothing. You are not appreciating things for what they are and indulging in precious time while you do have them. You have it for as long as you are meant to.

It's quite virtuous how life allows us plenty of opportunities to learn, adapt, react, and readjust to different surroundings. To expand ourselves as beings. "For every action, There is a reaction."

I believe we should question everything, broadening our horizons. There are always questions to be answered. Such as question all of why something may have happened and try to take a positive out of it, or find a beauty in the negatives of it.

All of it happens right under our noses over time sometimes without us even knowing it. There are always plenty of highs and lows throughout all of life, and always plenty of time and options to weigh out. The part it took me forever to learn is to weigh them all out correctly is the difficult part, you're never able to doge the bullets life shoots at you. Although you are capable of how much pain and suffering you let it cause you.

I needed to learn how to rise up from the lows, and how to handle the lows when I was high. For those of you that want to throw in the towel at times... DON'T! The situation will never be ideal, I have been there... I STRUGGLE DAILY. That is why I want to put this out here so you know you were not alone and you are not alone now or ever. These are the thoughts I have over a span of time brought to life in poetry. Remember someone else is always relatable, I want to inspire people. I want someone to look at me and say "Because of you, I didn't give up." These poems are for you to sink yourself into. People experience so much emotion in life happy or dark and a little bit of all is in this book.

A Christian Man

A Christian man will say he is worthy,
He will say he is a good person.
But what do his actions say?
A Christian man should not give his word, that he is noble
trustworthy and kind,
He should prove it.
When the Christian man then deceives by judgment and terrorization
to the mental status of others,
by making them feel any less of who they are.
A Christian man is not two-faced,
he is the man that he should be.
Not a man that he only wants you to think he is,
only when looking into your eyes as he lies.
And as he takes those steps in the opposite direction,
an indecent serpent appears.
A Christian man does not belittle you to others, to turn against one
another, to become what he is,
 in judging what they do not know.

A Dark Chilly Night

It's chilly tonight, but not winter cold, it is fall chilly.
Where it is just enough to have on sweatpants and a hoodie.
It's late, and watching the hot embers in the fire struggle to
stay alive after a roaring fire seems calming.
All of the sounds in the atmosphere and woods around you,
swallow your urges to over-think.
No, instead you zone out, daydream, and inhale energy for your
body and mind to slow down and love nature,
 In which the trees have given me to write all that I have.
Crickets tonight could drown out the sound of a train,
the toads singing melody's of harmony.
Stars cluttering the blackened sky,
for unheard, but hopeful wishes to be made.
The clicking of cicada bugs,
the sound of sand paper rubbing together when the wind blows the leaves.
The wind softly whispers as it grazes through the night.

A Mothers Fight

A kangaroo felt lonely
She would Rome alone and about
Till one day she realized
Her tummy is getting big
And hoped a baby would come out

She pounced around in happiness
Stocking grubs for thy baby during great
But a leopard was prowling
From near by
Looking for something to eat

Day after day the kangaroo
Awaited for danger to come
Finally one day the leopard
From the corner of her eye started to run

She took off as fast as she could
At this moment she could not outrun the big cat
She stopped and turned to stand her ground
But she knew she was no match

She kicked and fought as hard as she could
As the leopard thrashed and growled
Her rage for the baby was larger
Then the leopard's fierce and hungry mouth

The leopard finally gave up
And proudly walked away
While mama lay down wondering
If she had just fought her babies last day

For days she stopped feeling kicking

She felt like she had lost her joey
The only thing left was to rest and wait
for the only thing, that wouldn't make her lonely

Then one day, she felt a kick
And a push, he was ready to come out
The baby was there and as a surprise
He crushed mama kangaroo's doubt

She had her little joey undeveloped but alive
Mama carried the joey
Even through the fight
In her pouch the baby, happily survived

A New Leaf

Upon the life you seek,
Begin to see all the beautiful things.
The operator was within all along,
Turn the new leaf over,
Sing an intriguing song.
Eternity should be saintly not a sin,
Soon it will all sink into your skin.
Notorious for exotic life,
Of impulsivity to be found.
For this you'll become,
Keep focused and profound.
Keep your feet on the ground,
Your head in the clouds,
For what you seek...
Soon be found.

A Scary Dream

The path wound on and on, snaking through unkempt fields, and groves of uncultivated trees.
Wild with brambles and brushes.
I didn't care where it led,
or how scary it was to get there, as long as it was away...
 I didn't know what I was running from, but I felt there was so much emotion and terrifying pain in my heart.
I soon stopped in the middle of nowhere... lost. Bent over hands on knees, chest exploding, weak.
My legs were rubber,
When I looked up I saw a black figure standing beyond me in the woods... Realizing it was me, a terrifying sight of me at that...
That's what I must've been running from,
My destroyed self agony of all the pain I have been caused in life.
A destroyed disgusting run down sight of me,
but I couldn't get away from it all,
it would always stand as my shadow.
Then I followed my broken figure to a beautiful cliff side with great scenery and jumped, releasing all of my pain...
as I was falling I realized I was falling into fire...
that's when I woke up sweating and screaming.

Abduction of the Mind

Abduction of the mind comes frequently often.
We let good or bad, unforgettable moments take control over us,
as we re-play the scenes.
Naturally we are often taught to abandon things in life that are evil-like or unfriendly.
But we unsatisfying cling to that in which causes us certain pain.
Disregarding what is truly needed blocked by what we selfishly and foolishly want to work,
Enabling ourselves to love nouns, so fatal to us.
Like the water beating against the broken walls holding it back for if the water makes it through,
could be fatally unpredictable.
Our petty and stubborn minds feel it necessary to fix something,
that has already been broken, shattered, or destroyed us.
We became satisfied with a guilty conscience,
because fighting for ourselves seems so unbearable.
At the point of having the bad things constantly acknowledged and the blame is put onto you.
With no consideration of how one feels.
People sabotage each other and beat the weak down with every aspect until diminished.
Causing such excruciating pain inside and out mentally,
physically, and emotionally.
All of this which causes you to have a brutal war with your own mind. Feeling lifeless every step of the way, feeling there is nothing left to gain from this life and wanting to end it.
Utterly hopeless inside.
Unsure if you're able to take on much more.

Alcohol Is Temporary

3 olives with absolute,
I asked
I will have my drink
With a certain class
A drink to numb
The overwhelming day
Like the salt off the margarita rim
To taste the disdain
Pickle juice and jack
To get the buzz quicker
Take off the anxiety in my chest
Rip it off like a sticker

I then get this feeling every time I drink, and as I am writing. I feel like alcohol is a chameleon, It is disguised to be just the thing we need, when in fact it is exactly what we don't need, It is just a want on the front burner for our problems. I had always believed that liquor creates fun, and relieves stress, when in fact...
In the end it creates chaos, and amplifies everything overall. This "Pick me up" is everything but!
It only drags me down a deeper darker whole then I was mentally or physically in. I can feel the alcohol brand my issues deeper as I continue to nonchalantly throw more liquor down my throat. I wake up each and every time feeling the deep seeded guilt that blasts in my head, along with the atrocious hangover.

Are there limits?

Daring the soul to go beyond,
Boundaries are imaginary,
Rules are made up only in denial.
Limits don't exist,
So time is precious,
Extend while you persist.
Raising ecstasy,
Never missing an opportunity.
Never having to force anything,
That is truly meant to be.
But you do not receive anything,
That you do not earn.
To live it most fulfilling,
We need to be willing to let go,
Sometimes the life we have planned.
So as to have the life that is waiting,
To become intelligently realistic.
Not to assume what is for us
In future existence.

Ascending From the Coal

Diamonds of the rough
Compassionately cut
Smitten with the precious gem
Enrichment of brilliant rhinestones
Crystals bedazzle
Attached around skin for our decoration
Embellishing in the treasured stones
Invested work of the pearls
From the infamous aging shells
Opals glowing static colors
We wear these diamonds
As ultimate non synthetic riches
Careless expenses spent on rare ice
Instead of wearing these glorious gems
We could BE hard as a stone
Be the diamond
When we get a chance
Appreciate the coal
It may not be elegant, nor divine
Mined from the deep volcanic eruption
Created off the source material of coal
Developed the ascent of diamonds
So although growing as a jewel
Remember where you have been

Back To Life with Love

We have had our moments
We have had our doubts
We have definitely had those times
To rip each other's throats out

We have struggled
We have scraped
But I wouldn't do it with anyone else
Our hearts are entwined to never escape

One thing I know
Is I never doubt us
Forever we will fight
For our love, and trust

Not for one moment
Could I live without you
You are the missing piece
And to my brain the missing screw

You are the one
In every single way
Everything about you is perfect
I love you more everyday

Every second gets better
The time I spend with you
You're spirit grows upon me
I know this love is true

The life I spent without you
Was nothing worth it of any sort
Now I have every reason to live

Because of you there are no reasons to abort

I can look to the future
I can see what could be amassed
We will be our own family
Everything else lives in the past

I appreciate all the wonderful things
That you have done for me
Showing me so much support and growth
You have made me clearly see

Batter Up!

Take a step forward,
To the plate with the risks.
Do you take the swing,
And hope to god you don't miss.

Digging your cleats,
Into the sand beneath you.
They yell "BATTER UP!"
As your shadow deceives and protrudes.

The figure below you,
Stands tall and strong.
But inside your doubts, don't seem worth the shots,
But all it takes, is all you've got.

Reaching high,
Keeps a man on his toes.
Hold your head higher,
Don't think about the blows.

It's about playing catch,
And throwing strikes.
So hit the ball,
And dig your spikes.

Life is like baseball, you're scared or unsure.
If you refuse to lose,
Take a shot, at least you tried.
Maybe make a home run, it could be the cure.

So take chances, take risks,
A good team's promise "I'll never leave you alone."
Standing right beside you,
Let your team wave you home.

Believe In Yourself

Those who have known defeat, known struggle, loss, and departure,
have found their way out of the depths.
These persons have an extended appreciation, sensitivity,
and an understanding of life that fills them with compassion,
gentleness, and a deep loving concern for all that exists.
A historical way of such deep love, as sonnets were devoured
from broken hearts.
Wondering if love also has such true meaning and beauty to find.
Like this beautiful quote I once heard, "Like a bird sitting on a tree,
is never afraid of the branch breaking,
because the trust is not on the branch, but on its own wings.
Always believe in yourself."
Live by that.

Broadened Horizons

Turn your tunnel vision
Into broadened horizons
Accept that revenge
Is not the correct action
For karma will certainly reveal itself
Aspire to greater heights
Expand with lofty ambitions
Fearful, yet fascinated
Awed yet attracted
Let your feelings be powerful
Yet keep them on a personal level
Of being over whelmed and inspired within
Stay inspired with the delusional and exotic thoughts
Let your imagination take its course
Whisking you in the right direction
Towards evolution
Those selfish people with ulterior motives
Cut them out and keep your heart
Where you know it is safest
Self centered preaching
Their analysis is improbable
That your life is illogical
Forgive those and succeed anyways
For people are unreasonable
Faithful, Unique, different,
Is exactly who you are
Keep the trust within yourself
For you are the brightest star

Cathartic Zone

As the months and weeks wore on into spring
And one opportunity after another passed
I became more and more impatient with myself
Consistently dipped into the reckless

A comfort zone is a beautiful place
But nothing ever grows there
Nothing will become of what is not sought after
Surely the future holds all that has not been exercised
Left undiscovered

A restless yet cathartic experience
To venture along an extreme journey
Becoming a more delightful version
Of our disoriented self

That we know we can eventually be
For astray as we have reduced
Being reformed is never dilate

Change

Shifting for brighter revelation
Creations of change
Steps into new transition
Discover new abilities unclaimed

Switch the old roles
Begin a variance of yourself
Never play into same routines
Make revisions for your health

Seasons change quickly
Day to day life goes by fast
The old you hasn't become scarce
But much less of a devotion detached

Unexpected mutation grows rabid
Alterations in the midst
The metamorphosis is inclined
Inception is in soul eclipsed

Circumstance

Sometimes you don't realize the weight of a burden you've been carrying until you feel the weight of its full release. Be strong enough to let go, and patient enough to wait for what you deserve; because what you deserve is always waiting for you to embrace it, much of this takes growing to get there. Perception is our evolution to see the past as a blessing and never a burden, because all that occurs is designed to support our spiritual evolution on earth. We move as a fog through life that is created to hold balanced in between air and ground, choosing to rise above it or fall below is how we wake to the fog each day.

Comparison

We have to learn that...
The eyes are truly useless,
When the mind is blind.
Purpose is hidden,
Something lost we cannot find.
Love is a country,
We cannot defend.
Hope is a letter,
We never could send.
Life is a dictionary,
We cannot define.
Death has no choice,
We cannot resign.
Mistakes are inevitable,
We cannot regret upon.
Time is nonreturnable,
Like a ticking bomb.
Emotions run deep, uncontrollable,
As a wild creature of its nature.
Reluctance is a poker game, we can't skip any chances at life,
To be your own creator, and savior.
Secrecy's so bitter,
locked away in a box.
Tossing the key for the revealing someday again,
Seems so hard and unorthodox.
Even stars cannot shine without darkness,
There is always a caged withholding flaw.
Without pain there is no beauty in life,
Mistakes help us learn not to fall.

Confusion

Not all scars will show
Not all wounds will heal
You can't always see
The excruciating pain that someone feels

So maybe she laughs
Maybe she cries
Maybe you would be surprised
Everything secret she keeps inside

She self destructs
And falls apart
She tries not to show, Still no-one knows
She has a broken heart

Pushing everything
And everyone away
Deep down she will forever believe
Impossibility anyone would stay

She doesn't know how
To truly feel
How will she ever know the difference
What's fake and truly real

She's in the mode
Of self destruction
This dark paradise
Keeping her suctioned

Controversial

When lonely reside,
In what deeply hides inside.
Burns and stings,
Cripples your wings.

Controversial, Distant,
Rival yourself as you think.
Revealing, Concealing,
Unable to contain this feeling.

Presentation being rated,
Discretion becomes overrated.
Disorder, and Distortion,
Unfathomable like contortion.

Radiating explosive, Mind wants to burst,
Evil has a quenching thirst.
Intensifies losing control,
We all truly play our own little role.

As if falling from space,
Plummeting to earth.
Time passes searching,
For a sensible sort of rebirth.

Courage with Heart

Enrichment within the gracious hearts;
Supplying full gardens,
full of blossoming luxurious faith, trust, and love.
Withering from certain allegations,
that contain unauthorized distributions of the unknown theories people presume to create against others without recognition.
Although some are inconspicuous to the delayed gratification
people restrain from,
and portray fictitious and malicious acts onto those who are openly gracious.
The conspicuous of those with beautiful intentions in their hearts, will cure the poison, breaking the hate that has been enforced upon them along with harsh troubles.
They have been trapped,
and securely encased in.
Those with beautiful hearts will step in and lend a helping hand, rising to the occasion to help the less fortunate.
Wearing their hearts only on their sleeves.

Craving the Lost

Craving what has been lost with time
Though sourly never forgotten
The thirst for sweet
Or unhealthy attention
From long before what we got caught in
Pining longevity
For old flames fought with languish
Lovesick for harsh memories
Though scarce from anguish

Deafening yet Defining

We have this living luxury of beauty that goes unnoticed
We can only see ourselves
The silence is deafening yet defining...
We do not have the luxury as people to apologize
We make our decisions and act on them based on our surroundings
The silence is deafening yet defining...
Closing his eyes peacefully
After what seems like the tongue has been cut out
Unable to make contact of any sorts
You lye staring at the dark shadows with a wondering mind
The silence is deafening yet defining...
It is a peaceful reconcile you were searching for.
Yet the silence is still deafening yet defining...
Now you know
His heart doesn't truly belong to you
Your eyes cried dry and heavy
While peacefully
He sleeps.

Deep Spells

Tis no deeper spell, such as love
No deeper agony, than the loss of a loved one
No stronger pain, than that in which strengthens us
No larger disappointment, then deception
Tis no harder part in life, then editing your own production of it or the steps taken
Tis no better vision, then the sight of something new revealed
No stronger soul, then the act against violence
No better revenge, then killing with great kindness
Tis no bigger shown fear, then that of giving up on what is too difficult to achieve
No deeper weakness then just settling
No better gift then forgiveness
Most of all...
Tis no better life than that of love, ambition, and revolution with change

Delicate Rose

Eyes cry like waterfalls falling from above,
Delicate as a rose bud,
Peaceful as a dove.

Every soul has wholes patched,
Every heart has a chain wrapped,
Around that has been latched.

Apologize to the ones,
That have been hurt,
For the neglect,
Caused from loathing in self worth.

Rumor has it,
There is no such thing as magic,
What's to believe in,
Except for what's tragic.

The only thing scary,
Some people truly fear,
Is what they see from the reflection,
Appearing in the mirror.

Incarcerated to escape,
To something truly divine,
Searching for a dreamland,
You're unable to find.

Desire for the UN-reached

The journey of changing one's mind, heart, themselves entirely,
or way of life, is a difficult road of process to take.
When you for so long have loved, or find comfort and
relaxation, in the darkness.
The strongest feeling although is an intense and irresistible
desire for freedom, though unreachable it seems.
For that in which is unfamiliar, rare,
and strange, is yet so intensely marvelous.
Wandering alone is isolation, relying on
chance or an uncontrolled element in the details of life.
Searching for mental calmness,
clarity, composure, and evenness.
So behind every beautiful thing there has been some
outstanding kind of pain.
There must be in the end a discontinuation for the constant
desire of the things in which destroy you.

Doubt

Doubt will toy with the mind
Dwindling the ultra beauty
Of confidence staggering the climb

To step forth without decline
Will gracefully shatter
False unfaithful signs

Patience renders divine
Blood pumps on impulse
Body impatience mustn't incline

Do not resign
Nothing is worth a dividing line
Because your flaws do not define

In due time
Your heart healed
Will finally combine

In future time
Everything will connect
All will be fine

Empty

These memories like tight rubber bands
Wrapped around my mind
Sewed together
But completely broken up inside

Placed on a pedestal
Holding me still
Difficult to stay standing
With all the colors of personality
Disorders on me that have been spilled

So empty, no expression
Some can see right through me
Defenseless and broken
Yet satisfied
With the pain inside thee

Eternal Winter

After spending what seemed
Like an eternity in the dark
Cold and depressing depths of winter
With hard aching spirits
And exploding emotions
Finally today
I step outside
Into the warm sun
Melting dirty snow, torn up damp grass
The sound of birds singing
Creating shadows on the ground
As they glide, wings spread through the sunlight
A cloudless bright blue sky
Appears as I'm looking up to feel
The spring breeze, with its intoxicating smells

Exemplify

Introduce a genuine side
To those who are shy
To easily hide
Apply a welcoming smile
Build a trust
That makes our support worth while
To those less fortunate
Seeking dependability
Exemplify your craft
To show patience with empathy
Emphasize an initiative
To help organize their scattered mind
Share enthusiasm to fuel
The happiness left behind
Bring back the lost perspective
That anything is possible
Alternate that negative
Reinforce a positive intellect

Existence Is Not Questionable

Without love do we parish?
Without hope do we vanish?
Without talent do we plummet?
Are we nothing if pieces of us are missing?
Without confidence are we ugly?
Do we need someone to make us feel alive and worth something?
It would be nice if that wasn't the case... but no
You are not a fraction,
You are a complete master piece
All by yourself
You do not need anyone else to validate your existence.
You have a unique purpose about you that no one else has
The purpose for your existence?
Look in the mirror
You have it all right there

Extraordinary Perplexity

Extraordinary perplexity,

Baffling, and theatrical to the eyes but reposed on genuine feelings.

An enslaved imagination, without vowels of mercy, with shifting insubstantial mists of

detestable attributes. A prestige of false or fiction theories, we may or may not feel

comfortable exposing ourselves to. Even in the face of adversity their lives kindness,

at a time when tragedy dominates world affairs of any kind, it's easy to despair at the path.

But the true antidote is to restore your faith in humanity, and take the step forward even if it's alone.

First Love

Yearning for love
What words could never say
Eager to embrace
An eternal flame

Relentless passion
UN-denying, deeply intense
For long term commitment
Attached unending tenderness

Almost seems unrealistic
An enchantment to relish in
Sworn into endless magic
Embellish in the dizzy youthful spin

Cherish every moment
Of the apothic internal flame
Two worlds split, becoming one
Excepting all love that is strange

For You And I

Purified by your eyes,
Relinquishing myself in your touch;
Lavishing each other in love,
Forever in your clutch.
Steady with your caress,
Though my heart thumps eager beneath;
Calm me with your soothing voice,
While your body makes me weak.
Crafting myself around your positivity,
Together in solstice.
Creating and sculpturing a world;
For you and I,
Through all we will proceed.
Capture the beauty,
In every moment we share;
Cherishing every second,
For no other feeling could compare.

Furnished Canvas

Love is a Canvas pattern furnished by nature, and embroidered by imagination. Charm the road way through the racing anticipation. Advertising yourself to recover something out there that's bigger than yourself to believe in.

That uninterrupted innocence is so voluminous, giving the plentiful ponder, of recognition. A powerful, cynical touchstone, yet to express genuine emotion. Hiding beneath words and language, because we are afraid in the beginning of taking actions for the comfort ability will disintegrate.

Compassion is not a relationship between the healer and the wounded, it's a relationship between equals. Only when we know our own darkness well, can we be present with the darkness of others. Compassion becomes real when we recognize our shared humanity.

Goosebumps from Him

He looks at me
I grind my teeth
Wondering hard
What good it does him gawking

Pulling me closer
Breathing in my ear
Whispering sweet nothingness
I never thought I would hear

He runs his fingers softly
Up and down my goose-bumped skin
Grinning small at the happiness
With the heat of my blood rushing within

He breaks me down, weakened
By the arms he throws around me
Safe and sound within his realm
Home is now where I can be

He notions me come closer
Without attempting anything slick
"You are my everything," he says
Suddenly my stomach felt sick

This is a man that loves me
For everything I am
I realize its butterflies
And he is the perfect man

Haunted Innocence

As you gaze into a darkness, you imagine a certain distance between you and another life. A life that would come out of oblivion to greet you, as if it has really never existed or is undiscovered, most certainly UN-describable. Is it heaven or hell, is it just your insides crawling with fear. Putting deep unrealistic images in your mind. Look up into the stars, you see the tops of trees glowing. As you look afar to the blind side of you, it's not so dark at all. The moonlight beams down showing a gorgeous image to your eyes. Is this what it all looks like when I'm not blind from all that haunts me?
Is this really how the night sounds, so beautiful, when I don't let the silence cloud my mind with thoughts of gore and evil?

Does this mean I am coming out of my coma I have long awaited in to find happiness? Or …. is this just nature teasing me with an unfair presence, because I'll never see it again.

What is innocence? Or innocent love.....

If you can see it but you can't feel it... is it fake?
Or waiting for you to take the next step to let go and trust.

His Body and Mine

Lying beside his body
Warm beneath the sheets
I caress his chest my head is upon
While he plays footsie with me

My locks between his fingers
He glides his hand through my hair
Leaning over to kiss my forehead
I tell him my heart, feels in thin air

Our bodies become weightless
Together we became entwined
The emotional spirits erupting
And the sexual tension has inclined

No more words between us
The silence says it all
He extends his mouth to mine
From then was fanatical

Hour Glass

You can hope all your life that someday you will conquer and defeat
One of these days your heart will stop and play its final beat
Everybody's clock is ticking but they're unable to decide
How they want to spend the time that's left in their lives
A broken heart is blind, is always naive
A broken heart is dying from being deceived
Tic- Toc- Tic- Toc, the time goes by
Some waste away just waiting to die
For instance look inside pained eyes
You will see its dark inside
This is where all the demons hide
This heart will torture thoughts by day
And poison dreams by night
The exhausting punishment of wonder
Is a fear that blinds the sight
Paranoid of the invisible, abusing the brain with the unthinkable
These disturbances of feelings, screaming
Leaving us unstable

How Lost

She didn't know,
Who would leave or stay,
So she pushed them all away.
I thought you were different, but I was wrong,
I can feel you forgetting me,
I've been broken no longer strong.
I wish I could build up,
A world of magic,
Because my real life is tragic.
"Save me please!"
She cried out,
But everything was silent,
That came out of her mouth.
I don't want to die, unsure I want to live either,
I just want to disappear,
She feels like she is losing herself, no-one wants to hear.
As though she has been shoved away into complete silence,
Keeping everything to herself because of no sort of reliance.
Some truly have so much to say,
But everyone seems so far away.

Humble Yet Rumbled

Soar, yet humble,
Happy yet rumbled,
From all you have been through.
Stumble, and fall,
Laugh it all off,
For you know what you have to do.
Something borrowed,
Something new,
Nothing is to come,
If nothing is pursued.
Something old,
Something gold,
Treasure your being,
Don't always follow,
What you're told.
Believe nothing that you hear,
And only half of what you see,
If you can touch and feel,
What it truly is yourself,
Then it's certainly,
Meant to be.

Ice Breaker

The sleet between two people
Can be a bit shy and weary at first
But the ice breaker that cracks the glass
Brings two beings closer to converse

An intimidation settles
Knowing nothing of what is judged
No need to throw completely in at first glance
But give themselves a little nudge

We know nothing of what could come
Or what could surely be processed
From a little faith and trust
To give another a chance to not feel less

No one knows at first
What could be happening to someone else
Behind closed doors could be a sour life
So surely get to know the hidden course they shelf

Remove the general appearances
Explore what lies beyond show
Finalize a motion to work together
Facts of another life may relate you never know

An ice breaker between those
Could be anything civilly larger or small
Similarities you never imagined to grow
Would never be, if we judged all

Special people roam everywhere
All in separate life's with trial and error
Cherish others their qualities could be great
Judgment walks around in terror

Impossible Fairy tale

Love, An impossible fairy tale
The full devotion to a senseless dream
A shudder in his blood
Searching for perfect, taking extreme's
A sober and fearful gratitude
Mass tribulation of perplexity
Sheer Utopia
For all we search to be
If we are intended for great ends
We are called to great hazards
It's not just contentment
But a power surge in your heart
As if getting stabbed with a dagger
If I can't have you in reality
I'll settle for you in my sleep
When I wake again you won't be there
But the image I will keep
Sing me a lullaby
For the permanent sleep
For my mind tells me no
But my heart is in too deep

Indian Giver

You give something to take it away
Realizing you want it more
But do you need it, or is it the jealousy that speaks
When they have something you adore

The gift you gave was a need for them
But for you now it's just a want
The special quality of it is not as great to you as it is to them
It's not fair to treat and then taunt

It takes a savage to grant them then to thieve
The behavior is not forgiven
Telling someone take an apple, from my tree
They're delicious, juicy, and sweet, to do this is a harsh sin

You take a bite, then say PUT IT BACK!
To the stem of this beautiful tree
But it cannot be attached
The bite taken can't be replaced

It will never again be the same
That stem will now wilt
The leaves will lose their color
That trust will never be regained

Inspiration

Inspiration,
The agility for dreams
Sparkles, glitter, glowing towards growth
As if dangerous lightening strikes
But also lights the brain with beauty
Such charisma
Gaining providential success
Exploit towards rhythm
The beats on your skull
Exploding with color
Dripping with outstanding fabrication
The mind of a solar field
To harvest and empower
Resplendent winds assert aspiration

Intervention

A judging group attempting control, and deciphering of certain destroying factors, to

bring loved ones back to reality. Picking at the flaws, trying to unravel their meanings,

reasoning for the relapse, or the true pain behind all of the reckless commotion. Forcing

themselves upon those labeled as weak, with the excruciating criticism that is beheld.

The truth is without honesty only with-held in those that are within the experience of the

flaws created, and why it is the substitution all healer for them. There is no easy

condition to redeem from, especially on the conditions roughly enforced with. Those

will remain motionless to remove the urges of heinous acts to resemble what is needed

to be proven for change. The true change however will only become from those who

want it for themselves, realizing the distance pulling between loved ones and death as

well. To control the urges comes revelations cured.

Intuition

Imperfection is perfection
To A beautiful perspective
To be beautiful or creative
Divinely inspired
Peaceful and aspiring
Flaws, and Scars, Disorders
Distortion
With imagination
And a genuine outlook
Intuition with direction
Make the clock reverse
For this beauty
Is so wonderfully perverse
Attractive by the attributes
In which are held within
The outside doesn't matter
For it's only our skin

Let it go

Letting go is painful
To reach for what can be different
Even though we are doubtful
We shall live as though we are brave
Even when we are fearful
These are trials we have to face restless
And as selfishness and complaint
Pervert the mind
Then comes love with its joy clears
And sharpens the vision
Our personal work is to find acceptance
Within ourselves
And master the art of appreciation for small things
Wondering constantly of that in which had once
Caused us much distraught
Go confidently towards the direction
Of your greatest imagination
To focus and gain strength

Limited

The worst feeling in the world is knowing you did the best you could,

Yet it still wasn't good enough, starting to think nothing you do should.

Everything is spinning, world has disappeared,

Maybe one day everything will sit still and be clear.

For now my world is dark and cold, my mind is racing fast,

Of all the things that have burned and crushed me in the past.

The insecurities I have are washing me away,

Terrified that this way, forever I will stay.

Frustrated with these feelings I can no longer control,

What if this madness I'm forming, ends up swallowing me whole.

Empty, alone, deserted, neglected, but never once had I been protected.

I miss everything and everything doesn't miss me,

It all left me alone with nothing, to look past the tunnel for, to see.

"Remember you are not alone,

If you've ever felt this way guide your heart back home."

Love Shall Conquer

Love is rare
Love is strong
It shall not be toyed
Or strung along

Love shall conquer
Nothing nuzzled in between
Love is also fragile
The slate should start clean

Love is tender
It's not controlled
To seek solace in love
Never solitude enrolled

Treatment of grace
Love fulfilled
Growth for two embraced
Developed new thrills

Love is a patience
Love is kind
It can all seem surreal
Love is sublime

Loyalty

Always question where your loyalty lies. The people you trust will expect it. Your enemies will desire it, and those you treasure the most will without fail, abuse it. Some say loyalty inspires boundless hope, and while that may be, there is a catch. True loyalty takes years to a lifetime to build but only seconds to destroy. We are unable to detect it, nor control it, but once the truth comes alive, we are impaired for a decision. As our brain corrupts, bodies collapse, and hearts crumble, from betrayal and dismay. The truth can make us or destroy us.

Meaningful Time

Is time not a test for us?
Only to test our management skills,
How we appreciate and spend it.
You can never control it,
Speed it up, Nor slow it down.
Neither can we pause it,
Nor rewind it, For just a moment.
To bask in memories, or fix mistakes.
Time is special and rare,
We are meant to use it, as a valuable possession.
To make mistakes, and learn.
Becoming wiser to make meaningful choices.
For then, and only then after,
lessons learned, will we know what we want,
and need in the future.
What needs to be done to get there,
making it happen for us in the ending reality.
But never stop,
You learn something new,
Every day for time never stops.
There are no such things as mistakes,
Only intakes.

Momentum

Momentum can take
A long time to build
But only a moment to lose

Stay solution eccentric
Convert and execute
Build a primary system of clues

Challenge only appropriately
Use critical thinking
For creative results

Intellectual curiosity
Is an honest way
To continue for good cause

A collaborative assessment
For an adaptable future
Of excessive progress

The transparency
Of an undecided fate
Should never be at rest

Pleasures undiscovered
Silence unleashed
With full intent

To be content
With what has become
Is often time well spent

Stirring up the concepts, providing much suspense
Be still to the wind that sales you
To a place unlimited to more sense

Money Isn't Everything

Money isn't everything
But it pays for all
Money pays our debts big and small
It can also break us and we fall
Money can make us week
Or it can make us strong
Money can make us poor
Or it can make some above all
Money makes us evil
It also makes us sane
Money is a valuable thing
It also makes us vain
Money is not the root of all
But it brings us hope
To survive we all must break our backs
To earn the money that helps us cope
Unfortunately money is an essential asset
On a daily basis for us to survive
But money still can't fill our hearts
What we need most is passion to thrive

Muddy Waters

There lies a strange beauty
In the dead lifeless trees
Discolored grass
Darkened skies
After the winter protrude
Withered wood
From the consistent dampness
Muddy waters
Sop the cold still sleeted earth floor
Naked trees crack with the wind
Brittle colorless leaves float among the ground
It all looks so beautiful
Exploring for some inspiration
But I am freezing my ass off

Music

Melodies played with soul
Embellished with sweet harmony
Music that hits relatively to life
Regular rise and fall
In sweet intensity of waving sounds
Emphasizing tunes
With prominence to each note
How truly extrinsic rhythm is
To all instrumental narratives
Telling stories of all
Even without words
As orchestras summon attention
With exquisite brilliance
Such talents undaunted
Unraveling stories by chorus
Enthralling hearts with envy and hope

My Angel

To the baby I will someday have
 I am going to give you the confidence
That I could never grab
Uplifting, beginning, giving a life
You're my new born baby
I owe you all my might
My reason to awaken
Be happy and smile
A wonderful existence
The greatest reasoning to live
Making it all worth while
I'll spend the whole maternity
Deciding how to express my love for you
With appreciation for the rest of eternity
I'll tell you you're beautiful
With every attribute
No matter what they are
I will respect and love you
Gender, Religion, Straight or Gay
Mentally, or physically ill, Dysfunctional, etc.
No matter what the case I'll stay
I'll be there in the daytime
Evening or night
We will always be close
Understanding Each other
With absolutely no despite
Spoiled, Loyal
Shown much with confidence
Taking the steps
I wish I could've had, Yet with no regrets
Nor remorse
You and I will make it over the fence
You will be my pride, and my pearl

For I have waited so long to see
The beauty of someday having you
And how lovely you could turn out to be.

My Love

Those eyes are the moon
That lights up the darkness
And sorrow of my life
That smile brightens the path
Of which I walk down to happiness
So I don't get lost along the way
That laugh is the melody
That calms the beast of my hatred
And anger towards everyday
He is the beacon of hope
In my existence
The reason I can believe in love in this world

Nature's Course

As the snow melts away,
The life that was had decade,
Sprouts back up from the ground.
Trees grow their leaves,
Start planting the seeds,
Give nature the needs to grow profound.
The birds are chirping,
Water starts lurking,
As sheets of ice all melt away.
Clouds start to crumble,
Thunder has had its last rumble,
Sun peeks through, for a bright warm day.
Sand seeps through the toes,
Fresh air through the nose,
As animals hither from hibernation.
To seek out the life in which they have missed,
From extensive separation,
Universe can be both beautiful or malicious.

Natures Downfall

Melting and flooding
Back and forth
Natures love
Is a universal contort

Seemingly the flowers open
To bring in the Sunday
Thirsty but weeping, as the rain
Drowns completely overdone

The cactus thirsty
Off the sun will surely grow
Everything around wilts
And browns, dying without control

Nature's harsh challenges
Brutal against all
Witness what will grow again beautiful
Righteous after the downfall

Natures Mythical Infantry

Reconciling with the fog
Smothers the trunks of trees
Silhouettes hover
On the trickled, rained grass

Sky that is blackened
Like liquid tar
Still shines earth, with moon and mercury
The woodland sparkles

Twigs donating to the crackling flames
Quietened suddenly with the owls call
Dazzling presence upon
Of natures non-flushed noises

Mythical infantry
Thirsty to praise
All of natures varieties
Extends an abundance of beauty to man

An experience to die for
All that is retched
Is now a dull cadaver in mind
This moment is all that matters

Natures Palm

Weeping willows
Dampness in the clover field meadows
A mellow yellow
Becomes of the pedals
Turn of the seasons
Pleasing sounds
Crunching leaves
Barking hounds
Deer calling mates
Faithful skies
Swirl deep blue clouds
Birds float with no guide
Atmosphere of change
Walk the gypsy colored road
Rippling waters sing
Man fishes in his boat
Frogs hop and croak
Upon the water hyacinth
Tortoise heads peek above the duck weed
Swan sits upon a plinth
A couple on a park bench
Holding hands, looking beyond
These are the moments made for man
To sit in natures palm

New Sentiment

Taking in new sentiment
This air I breathe has a toxic blend
Pretending reluctance or indifference
When you are actually willing or eager
Saying no but meaning yes
Probabilities become folded
Into existence be perception
Taking a cosmic journey to precious eternity
As experience becomes the ultimate name we give to our mistakes
As the illusions we create
Fade and we learn a true reality
Create and emphasize
A life of passion, charm, leisurely pastimes, and cultivation
Of life's pleasures
A spontaneous journey to attract and move you
Excessive desires to take initiative to change
Leaving a conditioned life of security, conformity, and conservation
To gain an adventurous spirit within
Rather than a secure future with regrets
Unconstrained from obligation or conventions.

Night in little Italy

Wine and dine
A woman divine
Shoes shined
Her dress his tie combined

Dancing slow
Rhythm of the piano
Aphrodisiac food bestowed
Wine and desert behold

Love unexpressed
No need for words addressed
This night says it best
Ending undressed

Romance combined silhouettes
In cotton sheet sets
Connection's charismatic zest
True loves invest

Night of Darkness

Night of darkness
Day of light
Evening of sunset
Skies full of rainbow delight

Trees birthday blossoms
Waters roaring waves
Sun rising casts an enchanting spell
Glitter on the snow's gaze

Grass whistles songs with the wind
Clouds spin dark with thunder
Rain beats the ground like a drum
Fire crackling while the embers sparkle

Stars glisten in the charcoal black nights
Fog creeps covering nature's flowers in mist

Optional Marks

When you wipe someone off
From the face of your earth
Because you always gave
But there was never return

While the pain of relapse
Disappointments are inevitable
Suffering is optional
But never forgettable

We leave our mark
Forgiven or not
People always look back
Remembering what's been fought

Remember what's been taken
Lost, or returned
But most of all what's been earned
For so long what we yearned

Picture This

Picture me as happy as I was once before,
Picture that strong self being just once more.

Remember how I lasted so long through the dark,
Taking in each breath, one last rocky road to mark.

Picture me standing there happy, with flowers in my hair,
Saying the things that made your heart go soaring through the air.

Picture me as the greatest thing, that you've ever had,
Walking down a path that you know won't make me sad.

Take a kneel on the ground and ask just once more,
How can I make the indiscretions decease, instead they shake me to my core.

Loving the ways of everything, not giving up an inch,
If this was a dream I am in, the emotions need a pinch.

But who can take me, out of this mindset, of being so damn lost,
Only I, could do it, but it always comes with a cost.

If there could be a painting, of the emotions giving me a nudge,
It would be in both bright and dark colors, Spiraling into a smudge.

The dreams that are surrounding me in every inch of fear,
Scare me because when I wake again I should shed a tear.

Picture me as beautiful, and satisfying once to life,
Hopefully this fictitious person doesn't in reality use the knife.

How can someone that seems so happy, be at such high stakes,
It's because the only side she shows, is so easy but hard to fake.

How can I possibly get told I am so kind,
But yet still have this fighting war within my mind.

Tossing and turning fixing to shape,
This person feels as though her mind has gotten raped.

Of all that hurts her, yet is still a caring mind,
She stays true to her real being, of the one who is so kind.

So picture this, as this is a twist, Picture this mind perfect, with plenty love to spare,
The pain she is caused is something on the outside she will not wear.

Not on her sleeve or on her cheek,
But the love she wears all over, as people stomp on her in the street.

Plexiglas Prison

Staring through the Plexiglas,
Into your sad eyes.
Seeing you like this,
Just makes me want to cry.

I swallow down my tears,
Managing a weak grin.
You put your hand to the glass,
But I can't feel your skin.

I feel my eyes watering,
So I quickly look down.
Life is so empty,
Without having you around.

It seems like years,
But it's only been a couple days.
My hearts feeling so much,
But I'm not sure what to say.

It feels like we are imprisoned
Being kept apart,
But I just soon realized,
It's just because I lost your heart.

Protrude a New Horizon

Formally stand out
But informally rise
For those who doubt
Will endure surprise

It's the inner process
To guide and fulfill
All dreams are worthy to
Embrace with thrill

All things are possible
Untangling past knots
Shall protrude a new horizon
As you have rooted new spots

Engage the inevitable
Release what's withheld
Bring promise to the beating
Of what our heart won't expose itself

Pursue the Passion

Is a positive reinforcement just a hopeful yet fake reliance?
A gesture of unsure change, Unsure that things may or may not transcend or replenish for better. Even to persuade one to sabotage the doubt they have to pursue the passion within. Passion in which is hidden in the diminished wonders of life. To continue on sometimes we need false hope with good intentions to get us through hardships. Taking the unknown large steps to face our fate for the future, with hesitation lingering through our bodies. Prompted to indicate what choice of management to take among our lives, knowing not of what lies ahead, but can only imagine what's to come from previous and presented events.

Questionable Faith

Ever fought so much you achieved a demented peace within?

Ever got to a breaking point of confusion where you suddenly achieved a frustrated sense of clarity?

Does it feel like maintaining a literal sense of mind is more difficult, then a irreparably UN-Replenish-able mind?

Have you been tricked, by flying to close to what you thought you love?

Your prayers become bitter and all about blindness...

The amount you thought you had won in life you've lost in plain sight.

Squinting as everything you have once desired drifts further and further away.

Quiver in the Bitter

She can't run from what scares her
She quivers in the bitter steps she walks
She slurs her words
It hurts when she speaks
She swallows her burning tears
From running down her cheeks
For these frozen words
Are not easy to teach
Understanding her is tough
All of these secrets hidden
She drowns in her sorrows
Her love is forbidden
All of this melting
All of this vanishing cold
Is long awaited and bold
She's in love with the silence now
But is all forgiven?

Ripples

The leaves on the trees,
The grass on the ground.
Nature's evolutions are beautiful,
The changing sights and sounds.

Air is charmingly potent, Eyes are open wide,
Lying down while looking up.
Watching all the wonderful colors,
Collide and move with the clouds in the sky.

Water so still with a mirror reflection,
With a single drop it ripples. Nature can be prosperous,
Or atrocious still evolving each environment;
To which you choose, Each is their own,
A beauty one sees, could leave them happy or crippled.

Roads to Come

When all is forgiven my stars will align,
As excelsior takes a large, inspiration into my life.

My strength will be fully tested to take strides,
To redemption for clear sight.

I will be charmed into a delightfully unknown happiness;
As if in an elated world on thin ice,
Blissful, yet unethical because this feeling is so defiant yet nice.

For now it's difficult to understand and take in,
But for some reason I also think this could turn to sin.

Could this turn tragic, or is it just fate,
That I turn this sick feeling into love, taking away all the hate.

Distracted and deserted, I felt a recipe for failure,
Needed to push away from all, hoping to not again be hurt.

I can only hope this redemption is a path to blossom from
On my way some rocky roads to come.

Say It like This

I miss the way you look at me
Through those piercing eyes
I miss the way your skin feels
When it's rubbing against mine
I miss lying by your side
Waking up in your arms
I'd follow you to the end of the world
Just to be right where you are
The hours and days are slow
But I swear to you I will wait
Bound by love
Separated by heavens fences or hell's gates
The time fly's by when unwanted
I know we will be okay
Sometimes it's hard to believe
After many minutes
I regret never saying much more
I take a deep breath as I walk out the door
Next time I see you could be a while
Or never from today
I can't promise you that I'll be OK

So I guess I'll put it like this.....
I'm going to miss everything about you
Each and everyday
For you I will wait forever and always

Seeking Refuge

Sometimes the most dangerous place to seek refuge, is in your head. Release yourself and smile, even if it means grinding your teeth; Behind the bright Technicolor lipstick that covers the disdain. Shattering the mirror before you will not make your image disappear. It will only distort the reflection. To seek a way to see past the ingrained criticism that causes an immense amount of displeasure will slowly but surely, Ensure withering away.

Short Passage

The existence of premonition
results with a renunciation
Of abstracted unrealistic abstinence
Condemnation to adopt
Your own passage
Cryptic of the amnesty for remission
That of a difficult array
Barbarically abstract
Creating the musty muse
For a notable onlooker

Smoking

Light it up
Suck in the smoke
The cigarette burns
Into the being behold

A standing buzz
Believed to relieve stress
Alternate reaction
It's a call for distress

A sentence of life reduced
For an earlier death
Just for the withdraw
A fake cure to oppress, with a cigarette

Release of smoke
It blows through the air
Clouded black with each toke
The stench even stains the air

Masking your scent
Your taste and smell
Shading young beauty
Slowly working to hell

Smoking will fade
The gist of things
Only for a moment of time
Until the health begins to sting

A temporary settlement
Pretend it helps us cope
Chain smoking the damn things
But all problems continue to slope

As I write this... lighting up another

Snapped

All this time
She wonders why
The man she loves
Won't stay

Once it's done
He had his fun
He shattered her
Heart and brain

He plays his games
Says he loves her to her face
But stabs her
In the back

What's wrong with her
She wonders alone
While another woman
Takes off his slacks

When he comes back home
His needs already atoned
She holds him tight
But he walks away

He has something else
Puts her on a shelf
The back burner
She cries as he strays

She knows something's wrong
But she stays strong
Giving him her all

As she's strung along

Until the very next day amounts
Now it's all figured out
She sits and impatiently waits
For the confrontational downfall

One night he shows
She never comes home
He then realized
How much he loved her so

Soul of Fire

Reach into the fire
For the truth
While you watch
From the cold ignorance
Put my mind
Where I feel it's needed
Even if you don't believe it belongs
Grabbing the hands
Of the ones who suffer
And pull them into hope
While you watch the torture
Without a lending hand
I'll give my right to heaven
To someone who lost theirs
While you judge everyone else
As a demon who can't be spared
For I am the word of sacrifice
Who shall be heard
While you snicker in silence
Without an honest word

Staggering Thoughts

Swallow your pride
Choking on negativity
Acknowledging karma
Is stronger than revenge
Striving for greatness
While preparing for the worst
Devastation makes haste
As growth continues to make promise
Relishing for intense adrenaline
Abandoning common simplicity
The disconnect between the thoughts
And known reality is staggering

The Strength to Come

I feel as though I have blind eyes,
To sometimes expressing just what I feel inside.

You may have these feelings that will never be heard,
Because they say the things that come out of your mouth are absurd.

So your thoughts become a silent scream,
Left for us just to have bad dreams.

We cannot find ourselves a specific theme,
This scrambled mind is a rapid stream.

It's like the hardest jigsaw puzzle,
This life has left me to stumble and crumble.

Finding myself a happy medium,
Could be opposed to signing a death treaty for some.

Coping and curing seems like a magicians trick,
Between learning the magic, and ending it could take time it's not easy to pick.

My problem and solution will have to travel through my hands as well,
Some people give you advice in terms, as though it's easy to sell.

We are put through steps in recovery that seem so complicated,
Once we step out into this selfish world, Our strength is being rated.

I hoped these hardships are just temporary storage, to learn something better to come,
Thoughts are like viruses never fully disappearing but we can still enjoy the sun.

Sunny Days

As the sun calms itself
Dimming into the horizon
From a bright and vigorous high
Scorching with heat
To a cool colorful low
Disappearing beyond the sandy waters
That mirror and reflect it
The clouds spin dark
Stars surround a plump full moon
Sparkling and lighting bits of life
That has been darkened
To the night after day
Communication between earth's atmosphere
And nature is beautiful
The way they help one another grow

Term Oil

My rapid beating heart stumbles
Upon the blood rushing within my veins
My stomach is doing flips
While aching from impact
Each breath taken
Is becoming more insecure
As my body
Begins to shake excessively
The nervous butterflies fluttering
Throughout the insides of my body
Slicing me with the razor ends
Of their beautiful wings
Heart is on fire
Pounding as it melts
Dripping down
Burning the rest of my insides
Breathing profusely
As though drowning
Under dark waters
Too weak to swim
As though sour liquid
Is quickly filling my lungs
Hands trembling
Along with the rest of me
Like lying in the snow
Naked
Unable to get up
Frost bitten, So cold
Fallen to my knees
Ready to give in
Letting the anxiety take over
With only hope
That I'll make it through

The Cemetery

We last only as long as were supposed to finish our life's work. The work of nature is to make us who we are truly meant to be, and our creations and meaning to this world. Whether it's taking pain away from others, inflicting pain onto others causing conflicts onto others making them stronger with lessons of the weak. Learning to forgive, forget, move forward, and accept that Karma will takes its place. Those who are created to do wonderful things, making a better life, exploring in decorating the absence of what is missing. If life takes alternate routes, we may become deceased before our experiences have even provoked themselves into action. Beneath the meadows deep in the ground, some lye face up waiting for our second chance to kick into our spirit. Rising us for our mortal selves will be visible, yet alternatively powerful enough to attempt sending those a strong enough message in which never was understood from those who slipped away from us without noticeable grief. So many unknown questions and answers lay beneath us, supposing we will never truly know the case until we are compelled of what's rightfully meant to be. After our "Ending" we watch over our loved ones with compassion as a guardian angel, unable to do much but just enough to know there's always someone there to listen closely to our deepest prayers.
Here's to duplicity....

The Driving Range

Takes a deep breath
Lets it out slow
Relaxing himself to calm
As he golf's with a blow

Stands in position
Feet firmly positioned
Feet firmly placed
Checks his precision
Of the range and space

His pinky fingers entwined
At the swing he drives with force
As the ball flings
And his hips contort

150, 200
300 it sores
He hits and stands in position
Watching proud as if he scored

SMACK! As the driver
Whacks the ball
At bay 15
In Stone brook Wall

Take your shot ready or not....

The Hateful Love

How can you stand there and have no shame,
For the things that you've done,
And the people you have framed.
Framed into something,
That person wasn't before, but now ashamed.

You have now created a monster,
Self hatred nothing good,
This person once before,
Would have loved where they had stood.

Now they cannot stand,
To even look into the mirror,
Taking for granted everything,
That they once held so dear.

If once taken lightly,
Now everything is taken harsh,
So many things too hard to bear,
Want to quit, from all in which,
It sourly starts.

Taking these lies and hate,
Shove them in a pocket,
To save for later, questioning the reveal,
Only to wish you could put them in a box,
and forever lock it.

The Journey

As though I was a fish stuck in a shallow, rapid stream
Stuck and taking just short breaths, only to reach its dream.

A deep clear pond, with miles of length and plenty of good life to spare,
If this fish could only walk on land it would embrace the great smell of evening air.

There will be plenty of hard obstacles it will have to push through,
But then there will be worsened shallow ravines that it will have to pursue.

The fish wants to give up as it gets stuck in the part of higher sand,
It thought to itself if I give up now my life will never be grand.

Nature sees all the fish's struggles, so it starts to storm and rain,
Sending the water speeding down the stream, making the water higher to regain.

Regain its strength to flop around back into its persistent mind,
To get to the pond and live, clearing its corrupt mind.

The fish goes through struggle and pain finally getting to the pond,
It successfully gets to stop the life full of ruckus, and will finally see beyond.

The fish recovers from all of the hard obstacles it has to endure,
Finally having a recovered and recouped mind, to live a life that's pure.

The Mission

If life is a gift
Why is it so hard
To define and find
It's more like a treasure
Clues on a map
We have to combine
A pact within
To do whatever it takes
To sail abroad, no matter the stakes
An impossible mission
The escape from refuge
Find a reputable position in life
A compass with certainty
Optimism aimed in use
A new endeavor
Un-Anchored ground to seize
You only live once
Embrace it like a pirate
Enrich in the journey

The Ocean

Immense billows of waves
Brine waters sweeping the ocean floor
Fluctuating currents
Aged creatures in the blue galore

Deep in the rippling shadows
Lies a world unknown beneath
Tides will drag what's above below
Though what's strong, shall not sink

An ocean has so many beauties
Elements sweet and harsh
A flux of waves uncontrolled
Setting sun off in distance under stars

The ocean has many exotics
Ranging interchangeably
Stretching far and wide
Withholding mysteries, never to be seen

The Past

The past
Is never the best forecast
For the future
You have to try
You can't fail if you at least fight
Stick to what is sure
Redacting your heart
Will cause raw results
Access your outlook on loves agenda
Embrace without sulk
Restore a blend of ingredients
Too manufacture a relationship
Consuming that bond with trust
The bond will create future hope
Hope that is rich and definitive
Real grounds to firmly plant yourself

The Perfect Day

White lavender accented
With the breeze
Of another exquisite morning
Humming birds flutter
Towards the elegant butterfly bush
For the savory nectar
In which they lust for
The clouds drift by with bliss
As the wood pecker announces its arrival
With a sharp chirping song
The bird nails its beak into the tree
While the wind chimes hanging on the branch
Sway back and forth
Drumming against itself
Producing echoing music
Rabbits playing their love chase
Through the bushes, rustling the leaves
It starts to drizzle lightly
The deer take shelter under the trees that umbrella them
The day can go dark
But still stay beautiful

The Perfect Love

All I ever wanted,
A love that's true.
A love that's pure,
A love like you.

A love I know,
Will grow so strong.
Will work so hard,
And last so long.

The love I need,
The love I want.
The love that's clear,
And not just a taunt.

A love with hope,
The love I'll never have to let go.
A love that will last forever,
A love like ours I will let no one sever.

The love that is clear,
And never mistaken.
My heart is yours,
For the taking.

The love I need to survive,
A love without.
My heart would die.

The Perfect Rose

Out of the whole garden
 You're the most beautiful rose I've ever seen,
I wish to fully admire your beauty for eternity
And in return I'd cherish every pedal
 Every thorn
Every leaf
All the roots you have
Even when you start to wilt
I will hold you and pamper you
Until the last pedal has fallen
Even when completely detached
I will spend every second painting a canvas
 How beautiful you once were
All the beauty even wilted I still see

The Tree

I am a tree

I cover everyone and everything else

When it rains and storms

But when it changes seasons

And the earth turns rough

I turn ever so hollow

Shutting down, Shedding it all on my own

When the wind blows and it gets cold and bitter

A destruction of my nature, takes its course

I am then leafless and brittle

Sometimes it's good to get a little help you need to be nurtured and grow

The most beautiful things in life take the longest to blossom

The Vow

He caressed my skin and he sighed,
He knew the pain that was inside.
Looked up at me with a little grin,
Kissed the scars that I felt were a sin.
Looked back into my eyes,
With his hand on my cheek.
Told me I'm the most beautiful thing,
He's ever seen.
For this was all I needed and hoped for,
He is everything I desired,
And I'm finally everything he adores.
How could I ever live without him,
Along with everything else beautiful I've been given.
As he's looking at me,
Thoughts racing through my head.
Without this man I would be dead.
Then he spoke out again....
"I am not ashamed, nor appalled,
It just hurts to see others judge,
What they don't know is all.
So creative, exotic, generous, and loyal,
It's a shame the good things others try to spoil.
You're one of a kind there's no denying that,
Wouldn't have you any other way, that's a fact."
I'll never forget the day I first saw your face,
My heart had stopped, my mind was at a race.
Stunned yet fascinated, with the beauty I saw,
I laid my eyes on you, what it took that was all.
Before you met me, I was not right,
But things were really heavy, you brought me to life.
No other couple is quite like us,
This be pure love not lust.
I couldn't ask for more then you,

You're all I have got to look most forward to.
You and I truly have each other's best interests at heart,
That's how I know we'll never fall apart.
I'll love you forever, Now is our start,
These are my vows, until death do us part.

Time to Be Returned

If I would only learn to realize
To let go of the ones I do despise
The only way I can be free
 learning to let go of the bad
 Flee knowing to do what's best for me

Seeing the ways we always try
To make despicable people happy
Even though we always secretly cry

There is no way that I could be
Any closer to what is expected of me
I can't get away from these things I fear
Let's me knowingly take in
My growing times are here

The way that we can make our fate
Is to let our hearts grow and never hate
For the time lost with others
We fear abandonment
But we also try to hold on and think
Back on certain times that were spent

Should there be a brilliant time
That we all can take back our shine
Make it bright with all our might
To bring ourselves up and make life all right

To Push or to Pull

I'd hoped that we would find a place,

That we shouldn't have to change our pace.

For my racing heart can't slow to see,

The choices that there has to be.

If sticking by you was a painful choice,

I wish I would've listened to the better opinions voiced.

UN-Forbidden Tears

Tears streaming down my face,
Flow onto thy lips for a bitter taste.

Throbbing heart, erupting mind,
This broken feeling will leave you blind.

To get motivated feels like stepping on glass,
But in time this too shall pass.

Hope is not pretending that there's never any sorrow,
It's the knowledge that our troubles will be overcome tomorrow.

It's the inner strength we call on, to sustain us now and then,
Until our problems lie behind us, and we are happy once again.

Unwind

Close your eyes and listen to the rain,
Forget all the things that have caused you pain.
Smell the air, let the emotions flow through your mind,
All those feelings that kept you chained, let your heart unwind.

Spend your nights looking at the sky,
Attempting to get rid of this rough stride.
Thoughts when you pass away,
It'll be alone, and dark slowly fading away.

Never let yourself turn fully hallow,
It's a poison like nothing else, it's hard to swallow.
Experiencing the feelings of all the seasons, hot or cold against your skin,
Live life now before it comes time reincarnation sinks in.

Sometimes you think the outer body experience is staring back,
Would be very disappointed in the turn outs to be.

Walk Me Down

Hold my hand
Walk me down
The meadow of wicked dreams

The comfort-ability factor
Embracing the beauty side UN-torn
Etched deeply beneath

Walk this path
For the grass could be greener
With no trench for evil to climb

The silver lining
Beyond the stakes
Floats the current of all that's divine

What's Done Is Done

Day is over,
Night has come.
Today is gone,
What's done is done.

Embrace your dreams,
Through the night.
Tomorrow comes,
With a whole new light.

Staring at the ceiling,
Making friends with shadows on the walls,
Open your eyes and realize,
This cold feeling will thaw.

Life itself,
Is the most wonderful fairy tale.
Write it among ourselves,
Live wild on unleveled scales.

When the wind sends you,
 In the wrong direction,
Turn your sales,
 In your own perception.

Never Ignore,
The graciousness of life.
Tis a vast punishment for betrayal,
Don't lose the moon, while counting, the stars at night.

When Lightening Strikes

I wonder what it is I am supposed to accomplish,

or the greater purpose of these actions I pursue on a daily basis that I may only hope to

master the unparaphrasable meaning of one day, and the lightening like agility that

allows it to strike. When it doesn't withdrawal from combat in the first fight... It strikes

again. So quick to the eye it could be gone in the same instant. It is one of those

anomalies we may never be able to solve. One day the accumulated force of these hard

forcing currents in my life and all the tensions coiled within, will burst, flood, and sweep

from the planet like the disintegration of someone or something being struck by

lightening.

When We Were Young

Children building castles
Playing in the sun
Smells of sunscreen linger
Little laughs of splashing fun
Trampling through the water
Skipping flat rocks
Racing to the food stand
To buy colorful push pops
Seagulls flying with the waves
Kites gliding on string
Through the winds in clouds way
Pick up the driftwood
Write messages in the sand
Drinking juice boxes from a cooler
Digging holes with mom and dad
Hike up to the lighthouse
To watch the sun fall
Looking back when we were little
When we could have it all

Winter Delicacy

Snow gracefully glides from the sky
Floats, landing and sticking to what catches it
Building up on all that can hold

Listen to the silence it creates
While the snowflakes with delicacy
Touch base and melt away

Ravines push to flow
Beneath the crackling ice
That covers it like a sheet

The mountains landslide
Tumbles, smothering the beauty that surrounds
Becoming a white empty space

Snow is black and white
It can be peaceful
Or create devastation

Snow is luminous
When it comes to its nature
Though cold no matter the circumstances

Wisdom to Speak

Can it be that our world has no wisdom to speak?
No faith even in our lies
No sense of what's conceived
The rhythm that moves us
The power to grow
All the things we pass and miss
As we continue to for go
Fail to see the beauty
That lies ahead
Some minds won't let expand
Being as thin as thread
A life that is blind
Is truly undefined
Missing the true nature of design

Wish Upon a Star

I wish I may
I wish I might
Look upon the scars I fight

See them as a beautiful soul
I wish we all would see them
As unfinished goals

Goals that I will someday achieve
And that in which
Those scars almost made me to never see

The future of my full thrilling life
The scars that went deep
The scars that caused me strife

These scars show me now
What I couldn't do then
Wake up every day, without already feeling dead

My scars will now be
What keeps me alive
For I wouldn't be who I am now...
If I hadn't survived

You Weren't Here

While you weren't here,
I cried every night.
A million tears fell,
Still my heart wasn't right.

While you weren't here,
I did what I could.
Hoping against neglect,
My decisions would be good.

While you weren't here,
A whole lot got changed.
My life became different,
My world rearranged.

While you weren't here,
I gained some in age.
Things just went on,
And life turned a page.

While you weren't here,
I just tried to go on.
Knowing what didn't kill me,
Would only make me strong.

While you weren't here,
I had to be alone.
To stand on my two feet,
To make my own home.

So that's where I am now,
At this stage in my life.
Sometimes scared and alone,

But still coping with strife.

And oh how I wish that,
Things could be different.
That I could go back,
To change our time in the past.

To a time before,
You weren't here.

Ending

When nobody has cared for so long, It's hard to accept it when someone finally does.

I guess silence is the most powerful scream, when you're lost in the thoughts.

Do you know what it's like to count your breaths?

Breathing them in rough, as you regret their existence.

Finally when you can breathe in a sort of Lamaze and mindfulness, after the mind has wandered into the past, the future, or into a story that can gradually continue on impassive like.

I imagined the only way to hold on, was to find something to live for

But it isn't, to hold on you have to find something you are willing to die for.

Coincidentally we rapidly believe in perceptions of our own that can unconsciously misguide us. Although we all demonstrate a different sense of optimism that may be difficult to understand for many. But we ultimately need to live in a world of complex techniques, or else we would all be the same. Many have beautifully detonated, explosive minds of imagination and creativity. That is what makes life interesting.

Repair don't replace, we were never created to live depressed, defeated, guilty, condemned, ashamed, or unworthy. We were created to be victorious. Be yourself but don't discard the old, for you live and you learn.

What is a boundary if you need not to be trapped, boundaries should be held for a certain extent. Otherwise withstand in your way to cause gaps. Refer don't repeat, reflect and accomplish progressing with sporadic yet choice decisions only to succeed promoting yourself onto higher ground.

Go forth without default and live life to its full capacity.

www.ingramcontent.com/pod-product-compliance
Lightning Source LLC
Chambersburg PA
CBHW021410290426
44108CB00010B/471